STUDY GUIDE

Discover ELIJAH AND ELISHA

PROPHETS WITH POWER

FAITH ALIVE
Christian Resources
Grand Rapids, Michigan

We thank Deb Fennema for writing the first edition of this study. This revised edition incorporates updates and suggestions by readers and small group leaders.

Cover photo: ©iStockphoto.com/Michael Westhoff

We welcome your comments. Call us at 1-800-333-8300 or e-mail us at editors@faithaliveresources.org.

ISBN 978-1-59255-289-4

5 4 3 2 1

Contents

How to Study

The questions in this study booklet will help you discover for yourself what the Bible says. This is inductive Bible study—in which you will discover the message for yourself.

Questions are the key to inductive Bible study. Through questions you search for the writers' thoughts and ideas. The questions in this booklet are designed to help you in your quest for answers. You can and should ask your own questions too. The Bible comes alive with meaning for many people as they discover the exciting truths it contains. Our hope and prayer is that this booklet will help the Bible come alive for you.

The questions in this study are designed to be used with the New International Version of the Bible, but other translations can also be used.

Step 1. Read each Bible passage several times. Allow the ideas to sink in. Think about their meaning. Ask questions about the passage.

Step 2. Answer the questions, drawing your answers from the passage. Remember that the purpose of the study is to discover what the Bible says. Write your answers in your own words. If you use Bible study aids such as commentaries or Bible handbooks, do so only after completing your own personal study.

Step 3. Apply the Bible's message to your own life. Ask,

- What is this passage saying to me?
- How does it challenge me? Comfort me? Encourage me?
- Is there a promise I should claim? A warning I should heed?
- For what can I give thanks?

If you sense God speaking to you in some way, respond to God in a personal prayer.

Step 4. Share your thoughts with someone else if possible. This will be easiest if you are part of a Bible study group that meets regularly to share discoveries and discuss questions. If you would like to learn of a study group in your area or if you would like more information on how to start a small group Bible study,

- write to Discover Your Bible at

  2850 Kalamazoo Ave. SE
Grand Rapids, MI 49560

  or

  P.O. Box 5070
STN LCD 1
Burlington, ON L7R 3Y8

- call toll-free 1-888-644-0814, e-mail *smallgroups@crcna.org*, or visit *www.SmallGroupMinistries.org* (for training advice and general information)

- call toll-free 1-800-333-8300 or visit *www.FaithAliveResources.org* (to order materials)

Introduction

The Old Testament prophets Elijah and Elisha served God in the days of some of the most wicked kings of Israel. Their stories are in the books of 1 and 2 Kings, history books in the Bible that describe the reigns of many kings of God's people. In the time of Elijah and Elisha, God's people were split into two monarchies: the kingdom of Israel (consisting of ten tribes) and the kingdom of Judah (two tribes).

Though much remains unknown about the lives of these prophets, most of what we do know centers on miracles they did. God sent Elijah and Elisha to reveal his faithfulness and power during a period when God's people and their leaders wandered far from God and fell deep into sin. The kings of God's people were supposed to study the law of God so that they could live and rule by it, but many of them set up idols of the gods of other nations and worshiped them. These kings preferred to rely on political alliances with other nations rather than relying on God. As a result, Elijah and Elisha often had to warn the kings of Israel to repent or face God's punishment, and, in return, these kings hated the prophets and often tried to kill them.

As you can imagine, some of these stories are sad and painful. Human sin sometimes lures people to destroy themselves and the people around them. But these stories are not without hope. Though wicked leaders and the people who followed them had to be punished, there were always some who still worshiped the one true God. Behind the scenes and often through the prophets he sent, God preserved a remnant of his people from whom a righteous Ruler would come. Today we know that this Ruler is Jesus, the Son of God who is also the promised descendant of Israel's King David (see 2 Sam. 7; Jer. 33:14-16; Luke 2:1-14).

We can learn many lessons from these stories about Elijah and Elisha. We learn about God's hatred of sin and generosity in grace. We learn about the faithfulness of believers who stand up for the Lord despite opposition. We also learn about ourselves, as we see people in ancient times struggling with some of the same questions we face:

- Why does God allow bad things to happen to believers?
- Why does living by faith often challenge us to do things for God that we're not used to doing, or things we're not comfortable with?
- Why do evil people seem to prosper?
- Why do we sometimes feel discouraged even when things go well?
- Does God really care about the little details of our lives?

Some of these questions don't have easy answers, but we pray that your study and discussions will help as you explore them together in this Bible study.

The Ministry of Elijah, Elisha, and Other Prophets

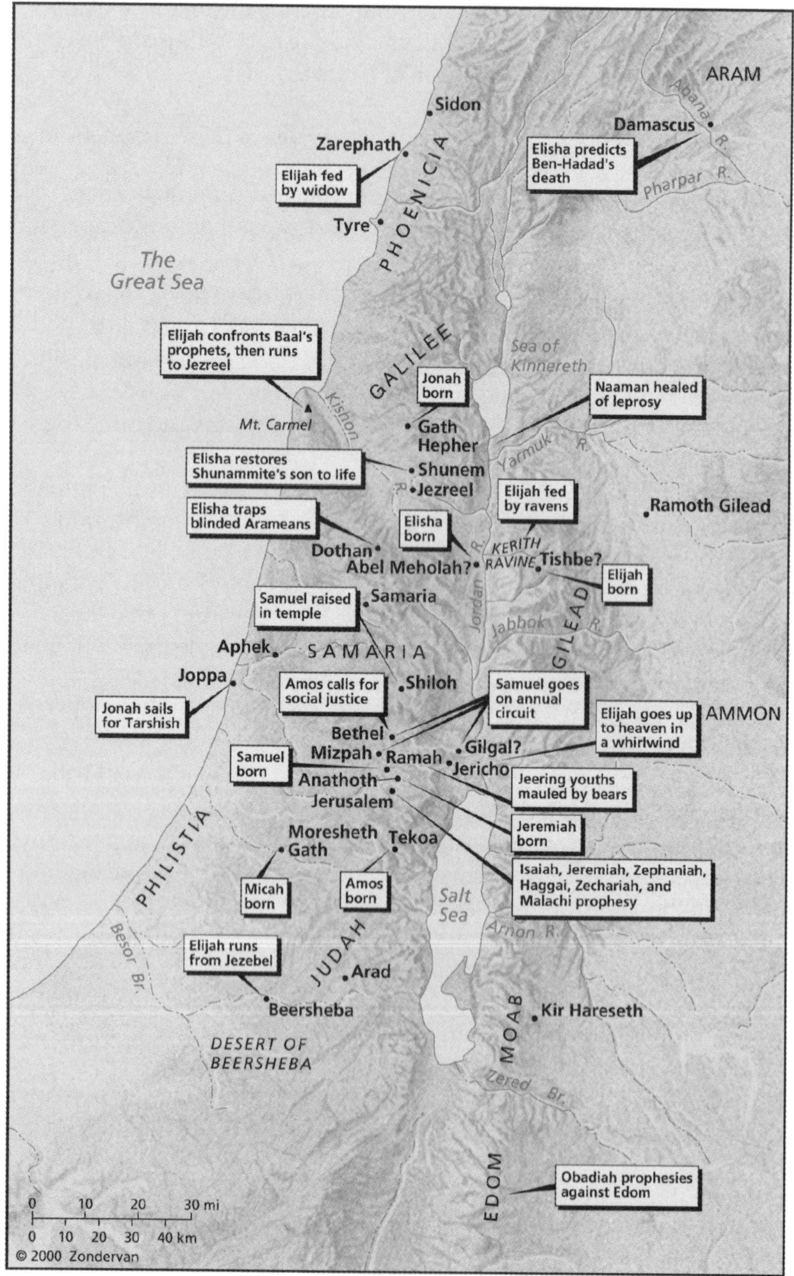

Glossary of Terms

Ahab—one of Israel's most rebellious and unfaithful kings. Ahab reigned in Israel for almost twenty-two years (874-853 B.C.). He married Jezebel, a worshiper of Baal, who built a temple to Baal in Samaria.

Ahaziah—a son of Ahab who became king of Israel after his father died. The last verse of 1 Kings 22 tells us that Ahaziah worshiped Baal and provoked the Lord to anger, as his father had done. He reigned only about two years, from 853-852 B.C.

Asherah—a Canaanite goddess, or a wooden image representing this goddess. Asherah was worshiped as the sexual companion of the god Baal.

Baal—This name means "master" or "husband" and is used to refer to several Canaanite storm gods. The Baal worshiped at the time of Ahab was probably Baal Melqart, the god of Tyre. Baal is also sometimes called Rimmon (see 2 Kings 5:18). When Ahab married Jezebel, princess of Tyre, she promoted Baal worship in Israel and tried to get rid of the worship of God.

Baal Shalisha—a region west of Gilgal

Baal-Zebub, the god of Ekron—this version of the god Baal was one of the most popular gods worshiped by the Philistines, Israel's longtime enemies in Palestine. The *NIV Study Bible* explains that the name Baal-Zebub "means 'lord of the flies,' a deliberate change by followers of the Lord (Yahweh) to ridicule and protest the worship of Baal-Zebul ('Baal the Prince'), a name known from ancient Canaanite texts." Ekron, a major city of the Philistines, was located about 25 miles (40 km) west of Jerusalem.

Baasha—a wicked king of Israel who reigned for twenty-four years. He destroyed Jeroboam's family but also walked "in the ways of Jeroboam and in his sin, which he had caused Israel to commit" (1 Kings 15:34). As a result, Baasha's family was also punished (16:1-13).

Ben-Hadad—a king of Aram who often battled and laid siege to Israel during the reigns of Ahab and his son Joram (1 Kings 20; 2 Kings 3:1; 5:1; 6:8, 24). Scholars note that this was Ben-Hadad II in the line of Aramean kings. He was later murdered by Hazael (2 Kings 8:7-15).

Bethel—an important city in the history of Israel. Jacob (whom God renamed Israel) had a vision of God at this site, receiving a promise that God would watch over him and never leave him. So Jacob set up a pillar there and named the place Bethel, which means "house of God" (Gen. 28:10-19; 35:14-15). Later in Israelite history the people set up the Lord's tabernacle (tent) for the ark of the covenant at Bethel, making it the site of God's presence in the land (Judg. 20:26-28). After the kingdom split into ten northern tribes (Israel) and two southern tribes (Judah), King Jeroboam of Israel again made Bethel a center for worship, setting up a golden calf there to be worshiped as God (1 Kings 12:28-29).

company of the prophets—a community of believers dedicated to experiencing God and preserving faith in the midst of Israel's widespread unfaithfulness. The *NIV Study Bible* notes that "the relationship of the Lord's great prophets (such as Samuel, Elijah, and Elisha) to these communities was understandably a close one," with these prophets "probably being their spiritual mentors." Further, "during the days of Elijah and Elisha, companies of prophets were located at Bethel [2 Kings 2:3], Jericho (v. 5), and Gilgal (4:38)."

double portion—the measure of inheritance given to a family's eldest son, who then also became responsible for the welfare of his father's dependents and related property. Other sons each received half as much as the eldest. (See Deut. 21:15-17.)

elders—leaders of the city, venerated for wisdom that comes with age and life experience.

Elijah—the Old Testament prophet sent by God to oppose Baal worship among God's people. In particular, Elijah stood against King Ahab and his rebellious family for their worship of Baal and other false gods. Kings and priests in Israel were supposed to serve as official representatives of the Lord, leading the people in faithfulness to God. But since the days of Jeroboam that had not happened in Israel, reports the *NIV Study Bible;* so "the Lord sent Elijah (and after him Elisha) to serve as his representative (instead of king and priest), much as Moses had done long ago." Elijah's name means "the LORD is my God."

Elisha—the prophet who carried on the work of Elijah in Israel, bringing God's Word to the people. Elisha's name means "God is salvation" or "God saves," describing the essence of his ministry.

Gilgal—see **company of the prophets**.

Hazael—God used this murderous king of Aram to punish Israel for its unfaithfulness (2 Kings 8:7-15, 28-29; 10:32-33; 13:3, 22-23). Hazael murdered King Ben-Hadad of Aram (8:15) and was succeeded by a son who was also named Ben-Hadad (13:24).

Hittites—descendants of an ancient Hittite empire that flourished before 1200 B.C. These people lived in city-state kingdoms mainly to the north of Aram.

Horeb (Mount Horeb)—also called Mount Sinai, this peak is located in the desert about 250 miles (400 kilometers) south of Beersheba. At Mount

Sinai, God spoke to Moses from a burning bush (Ex. 3:1-2) and gave his people the Ten Commandments (Ex. 19-20). The people also camped there for about two years to become established as a nation under God's covenant with them (Num. 10:11-13; Deut. 1:6; 5:2). Elijah traveled to this place while fleeing from Jezebel for his life (1 Kings 19:3-8).

Israel—the name commonly used in the Bible to refer to God's chosen people, the descendants of Jacob (whom God renamed Israel—Gen. 32:28). This name originally referred to all twelve tribes descended from the sons of Jacob, but after 930 B.C., when the kingdom split into ten northern tribes and two southern tribes, the name usually referred to the ten northern tribes. The two southern tribes, Judah and Benjamin, became known as the kingdom of Judah.

Jehoshaphat—a king of Judah who reigned during the time of Ahab and his sons. He was considered a faithful, godly king (1 Kings 22:41-44), but he became connected with Ahab's family through the marriage of his son and a daughter of Ahab (2 Kings 8:16-19, 25-27). On at least two occasions Jehoshaphat helped Ahab and his son Joram fight against their enemies (1 Kings 22; 2 Kings 3).

Jehu—a commander of Israel's army who was anointed king in order to bring God's punishment on the remaining family of Ahab (2 Kings 9:1-10).

Jericho—formerly an ancient Canaanite city that was destroyed when the Lord first led the Israelites into the promised land (Josh. 6). At that time Joshua pronounced a curse against anyone who planned to rebuild the city. About 550 years later, during the reign of Ahab, "Hiel of Bethel rebuilt Jericho" at the cost of his firstborn and youngest sons, "in accordance with the word of the LORD spoken by Joshua" (1 Kings 16:34). During the ministry of Elijah and Elisha, a company of the prophets took up residence there (2 Kings 2:5, 15).

Jeroboam—first king of the northern kingdom of Israel (ten tribes). He set up two golden calves for the people to worship, saying, "Here are your gods, O Israel, who brought you up out of Egypt" (1 Kings 12:28). For these and other sins against God and the people, Jeroboam and his family were punished (14:1-20; 15:25-30).

Jezebel—wife of Ahab and daughter of a priest-king of Tyre and Sidon. She promoted the worship of Baal and Asherah, her father's gods, in the land of Israel and tried to kill all of God's prophets.

Jezreel—a city about 22 miles (35 kilometers) southeast of Mount Carmel and about the same distance north of Samaria. Ahab kept a second palace there (see 1 Kings 21:1).

Jordan River—well known as the river that stopped flowing so that the people of Israel could cross on dry ground when they entered the promised land (Josh. 3-4). Elijah and Elisha also crossed the Jordan on dry ground on the day Elijah went up to heaven in a whirlwind and Elisha became his successor as prophet of the Lord (2 Kings 2:7-14).

Judah—the name commonly used to refer to the two southern tribes (Judah and Benjamin) of the divided kingdom of Israel. See **Israel**.

Mount Carmel—The Hebrew word for *Carmel* (*karmel*) means "fertile land" or "fruitful land," describing the lush vegetation on this mountain ridge near the Mediterranean Sea.

Obadiah—This Hebrew name meaning "servant of the LORD" is given to at least twelve men in the Old Testament. Scholars suggest that an ancient seal that reads "To Obadiah servant of the King" may have belonged to the administrator of Ahab's palace (see 1 Kings 18:3).

Philistines—longtime enemies of Israel, these people occupied the land near the Mediterranean Sea to the west of Judah.

sackcloth—coarse cloth usually made from the hair of goats and worn as a sign of mourning or repentance. It was usually worn next to the skin and occasionally as a robe.

sacred stone—a stone pillar that represented an idol god. God prohibited the use of sacred stones in Exodus 23:24 and Leviticus 26:1.

Samaria—capital city of the northern kingdom of Israel. This name sometimes also describes the entire region of the northern kingdom.

seah—a measure equaling about 7 quarts (7.3 L).

shekel—a monetary unit weighing about 2/5 of an ounce (11 g).

talent—a monetary unit weighing about 75 pounds (34 kg).

Lesson 1

1 Kings 17

Power over Life and Death

Additional Related Scriptures

Deuteronomy 10:12-19
1 Kings 16:31; 18:16
2 Kings 4; 13:21
Isaiah 55:6-11
Luke 7:11-17; 8:53-56
1 Corinthians 15
1 Thessalonians 4:13-18
James 5:16-18

Introductory Notes

Ahab was king of Israel from 874-853 B.C. The verses preceding this chapter tell us that Ahab "did more to provoke the LORD, the God of Israel, to anger than did all the kings of Israel before him" (1 Kings 16:33). Ahab married Jezebel, who worshiped Baal, a false god of fertility and crops who was believed to control the weather. Ahab followed his wife in worshiping Baal. He also set up Asherah poles, dedicated to a goddess associated with Baal. Elijah, the prophet of God, appears on the scene with little introduction.

1. ***1 Kings 17:1-6***

   a. What do we learn about Elijah in these verses?

   b. What does Elijah tell Ahab?

   c. How does the Lord provide for Elijah?

2. *1 Kings 17:7-12*

   a. Where does the Lord tell Elijah to go next? Why?

   b. Describe the widow's situation.

   c. How does she respond to Elijah?

3. *1 Kings 17:13-16*

   a. What message does Elijah bring from the Lord?

   b. How does the Lord provide for Elijah and the woman?

4. *1 Kings 17:17-24*

   a. To what does the woman attribute her son's death?

   b. How is her son's life restored?

   c. How does the widow respond?

   d. Why do you think God first saved the lives of the widow and her son by providing oil for them and then allowed the boy to die?

   e. How does this miracle reveal a power of God that is different from God's provision of oil?

Questions for Reflection

Have there been times in your life when you've been challenged to obey God in faith? What was the outcome?

Why do you think God asks us to take steps of faith without knowing the outcome?

Have there been times in your life when your faith has grown because of God's help? Has your faith also grown at times when God allowed something bad to happen? Explain.

Lesson 2

1 Kings 18

Who Is the One True God?

Additional Related Scriptures

Exodus 19; 20:3-4, 7; 29:38-41; 34:6-7
Leviticus 24:10-16
Deuteronomy 6:4-19; 10:20; 13:12-18
Joshua 23:6; 24:14-26
1 Kings 17:1; 19:10, 14, 18
2 Kings 22-23
2 Chronicles 2:4
Jeremiah 4:1-2
Malachi 3:1-5
Matthew 5:38-48; 6:24, 33; 10:37-39
1 Corinthians 10:31-11:1
Ephesians 4:15

Introductory Notes

This lesson covers one of most dramatic stories in the Bible. Elijah calls for a showdown between the Lord, the God of Israel, and Baal, the Canaanite god to whom Ahab and Jezebel have set up a fertility religion among God's people. The land has suffered from a long drought at God's command, showing that Baal has no power over the weather or agriculture. Now the people are at a crossroads in their life as a nation, and it's time to choose whether they will follow or reject God.

1. *1 Kings 18:1-6*

   a. What does the Lord say to Elijah?

   b. Who is Obadiah, and what does he do?

2. *1 Kings 18:7-15*

   a. What is Obadiah's concern?

   b. What does Elijah promise Obadiah?

3. *1 Kings 18:16-24*

   a. Why would Ahab call Elijah a "troubler of Israel"?

   b. What challenge does Elijah present? Why?

   c. How do Ahab and the people respond?

4. *1 Kings 18:25-29*

   a. How do the prophets of Baal approach their god?

   b. What is Baal's response?

5. *1 Kings 18:30-39*

   a. How does Elijah approach his God?

   b. What is the Lord's response? How do the people respond now?

6. *1 Kings 18:40-46*

   a. What happens to the prophets of Baal?

b. What does Elijah do next?

c. Why do you think God finally sends rain?

Questions for Reflection

In what situations today do we face a choice between following the true God and wandering off to follow other gods?

If someone wants to lead you into doing something that goes against God's law, are you prepared to respond? How will you present the truth in love for the sake of God's glory?

Think about some of the works of God in your life. Maybe you wandered and God nudged you to turn back. Maybe you were spared from a series of events that could have ruined you. Maybe you were stuck in a disaster, and God pulled you out. How can you use life stories like these to tell others about God's love and care for you?

Lesson 3

1 Kings 19

Never Alone

Additional Related Scriptures

Genesis 7:4, 12
Exodus 3:1; 19:1-20:21; 24:13; 33:11
Numbers 10:11-13
Deuteronomy 1:6; 5:2; 9:9, 11
2 Kings 8-10
Matthew 4:1-11

Introductory Notes

After the dramatic revelation of God's power on Mount Carmel (1 Kings 18; lesson 2), we might think Elijah would move quickly to rout the worship of false gods from among God's people and rally them to serve the one true God. But in this next episode of Elijah's story we find a fearful, worn-out prophet who feels alone and dejected.

Like all of us at times, Elijah needs encouragement and a nudge of correction from the Lord. This glimpse of the great prophet Elijah as a weak vessel who depends totally on God can give us encouragement in our own journey of faith. Through additional demonstrations of surprising power, the Lord assures Elijah—and us—that his beloved followers are never alone.

1. *1 Kings 19:1-9a*

   a. How does Queen Jezebel threaten Elijah?

   b. How does Elijah react?

c. How does God take care of Elijah?

d. What is Elijah's destination? How is it described?

2. *1 Kings 19:9b-18*

a. Why is Elijah discouraged?

b. Why do you think the Lord sends the wind, earthquake, and fire?

c. How does the Lord make his presence known? Why?

d. What does Elijah's response to the voice tell us about him?

e. What instructions does the Lord give to Elijah, and what will happen as a result?

f. How does all this show Elijah that he really is not alone?

3. *1 Kings 19:19-21*

   a. What does Elijah do when he finds Elisha? What does Elisha take this to mean?

   b. Why do you think Elisha slaughters his oxen?

Questions for Reflection

What do we learn about God in these events of Elijah's life?

What do these passages teach us about the worship of God and about faithful service for the Lord?

What words would you use to describe God? How do these stories affect your idea of who God is, how God cares for you, and how you can present God to others?

Lesson 4

1 Kings 21

God Punishes Sin

Additional Related Scriptures

Leviticus 24:13-16
Deuteronomy 17:6
Joshua 13-22
1 Kings 14:10-11; 15:25-16:13; 19:17; 20:1-43; 22:34-38, 51
2 Kings 1:16-17; 9:26, 30-37

Introductory Notes

In this lesson we focus on an episode that brings Elijah back to Ahab—to call him to account for shedding the blood of an innocent landowner. Here, as in many other Bible passages, God makes it clear that sin must be punished. As we reflect on this event in the life of God's people, let's note that none of us is above sinful maneuvering to get our own way, even though we may not commit outright murder to do it. As God's people today, we can give thanks for Jesus' death on our behalf to pay for all our sins. He paid the price for us so that we can have new life and begin to serve God faithfully.

Note: You may wish to read 1 Kings 20 on your own with the help of a study Bible. That passages reports how Ben-Hadad, the king of Aram, attacked Samaria, Ahab's capital in Israel. Scholars have discovered that this happened around 857 B.C. In the first attack, Ahab's army overpowered their enemy, as God's prophet had predicted (20:13). When the Arameans attacked again the following spring, Israel again won, but King Ahab freed the opposing king against God's intentions (20:42). So God sent a prophet to warn Ahab that his life and nation were in danger (see 20:35-43). In our passage for this lesson, we learn of another incident in which Ahab disobeys God.

1. 1 Kings 21:1-6

a. Why does Ahab want Naboth's vineyard?

b. Why does Naboth refuse Ahab's offer?

c. How does Ahab react?

2. *1 Kings 21:7-16*

   a. How does Jezebel address the problem? Describe her attitude and treatment of the king.

   b. What plan does she devise?

   c. What happens to Naboth?

3. *1 Kings 21:17-24*

a. What charges does Elijah bring against Ahab?

b. How will Ahab be punished? Why?

c. What will happen to Ahab's descendants? To Jezebel?

4. *1 Kings 21:25-29*

a. How does the author describe Ahab here?

b. How does Ahab respond to Elijah's words? What does God do as a result?

c. What is the purpose of these prophecies through Elijah?

Questions for Reflection

What do we learn about sin from this story?

What does this story teach us about God and about ourselves?

How can it help us share the truth and love of God with others?

Lesson 5

2 Kings 1:1-2:18

Passing the Mantle

Additional Related Scriptures

Joshua 3-4
2 Samuel 8:2
1 Kings 19:19-21
1 Kings 22:37, 51-53
2 Kings 3:4-5; 6:16-17; 13:14
Zechariah 13:4
Malachi 4:5-6
Matthew 3:4

Introductory Notes

This lesson covers the end of Elijah's ministry and the beginning of Elisha's. The biblical narrative hasn't mentioned Elisha since his call to succeed Elijah as prophet (1 Kings 19:19-21). The transition takes place with Elijah's amazing ascent to heaven.

Before passing along the mantle of prophet-leadership, however, Elijah must deal with Ahab's son Ahaziah, who has become king in his father's place. Though Ahab is dead (1 Kings 22:37), the influence of his rebellion against God remains in Israel. Like his father, Ahaziah provokes God to anger by worshiping Baal (22:51-53).

Many changes begin taking place in Israel after Ahab's death, and in these we see the hand of God bringing punishment as well as faithful care for his people. The neighboring nation of Moab rebels against Israel's power politics, the reign of Ahaziah ends quickly, and Elisha inherits the role of being the Lord's prophet in a time of entrenched wickedness.

1. *2 Kings 1:1-8*

   a. What has happened to King Ahaziah? Whom does Ahaziah want to consult?

   b. What message does the Lord send? Why?

c. How does Ahaziah respond?

2. *2 Kings 1:9-18*

a. How does the king try to approach Elijah? What happens?

b. Why is the life of the third captain spared?

c. How does Elijah's message come true?

3. *2 Kings 2:1-6*

a. What major event is about to take place?

b. What does Elijah tell Elisha to do? What does Elisha's answer reveal about his character?

4. *2 Kings 2:7-12*

a. How are Elijah and Elisha able to cross the Jordan River?

b. What does Elisha ask of Elijah? Why might Elisha ask this?

c. How does Elijah go to heaven, and how does Elisha respond?

5. *2 Kings 2:13-18*

a. What does Elisha receive?

b. How does Elisha get across the river?

c. What do the prophets offer to do, and how does Elisha respond?

Questions for Reflection

What has this lesson helped you learn about God? About serving God? About trusting God's Word and listening to God's prophets (those who bring God's Word to us)?

Are there any things that need to change in your life as you think about applying this lesson to your everyday living? If so, commit to making those changes, asking God for the strength to do so.

What can you share from this lesson to help someone else learn about and grow closer to God?

Lesson 6

2 Kings 2:19-3:27

Bringer of God's Word

Additional Related Scriptures

Leviticus 26:21-22
Deuteronomy 7
1 Kings 12:25-14:20; 22:41-47
2 Chronicles 18:1; 21:4-6

Introductory Notes

The events cited at the beginning of this lesson deliver a strong message that defines Elisha's ministry: the prophet encourages people in need and defends God's holy name. Then, in a story about Moab's revolt we discover that Elisha brings God's message to three allies—the kings of Israel, Judah, and Edom—but only out of respect for the king of Judah. Elisha makes clear that he would not otherwise help the king of Israel, who has continued to lead the people away from God. The Lord miraculously helps the three kings, and they follow God's instructions. In all of these events Elisha is affirmed as the Lord's prophet—the bringer of God's Word for God's people.

1. *2 Kings 2:19-25*

   a. What is wrong with the water in the city? How does Elisha handle this problem?

   b. What is wrong with the youths' treatment of Elisha? How does Elisha handle this problem?

2. *2 Kings 3:1-3*

Describe the new king of Israel. With whom is he compared?

3. *2 Kings 3:4-8*

 a. What does King Mesha of Moab do?

 b. How does King Joram respond, and who helps him? Why?

4. *2 Kings 3:9-20*

 a. In what predicament do the kings find themselves?

 b. How does Elisha get involved?

c. What does God tell the kings through Elisha? What happens?

5. *2 Kings 3:21-27*

   a. What do the Moabites think when they see all this? What do they do in response?

   b. How thorough is Moab's defeat?

   c. What does the king of Moab resort to?

Questions for Reflection

What do we learn about God from these stories?

What do we learn about Elisha's work as a prophet?

What "easy thing" might the Lord do for you? Maybe it's something you find impossible to do in your own strength. Are you asking the Lord to help you with the challenges in your life?

Lesson 7

2 Kings 4:1-44; 8:1-6

God's Mercy and Care

Additional Related Scriptures

Genesis 18:10-12
Leviticus 23:15-17; 25:39-43
Deuteronomy 15:12
1 Samuel 1:1-20
2 Kings 2:3, 5
2 Chronicles 2:4
Nehemiah 5:1-8
Matthew 6:30-34; 14:13-21; 15:29-39
Luke 1:1-2:7
Romans 8:28

Introductory Notes

Our passages for this lesson focus on four miracle stories about God's mercy and care for his people in their everyday lives. These stories show that God works through his people to help others in need. The miracles of Elisha also have a common theme—life overcomes death—and they give a foretaste of the ministry and the resurrection power of Jesus. In addition, they point forward to eternal life with God, in which people no longer fear slavery, starvation, death, or separation.

1. 2 Kings 4:1-7

a. What problem do the widow and her sons face?

b. How is the problem solved?

2. *2 Kings 4:8-17*

a. What does the Shunammite woman want to do for Elisha?

b. How does God reward the woman in this story?

3. *2 Kings 4:18-37*

a. What happens to the boy?

b. What does his mother do? Why?

c. How is the boy revived?

4. *2 Kings 4:38-41*

a. What's wrong with the stew?

b. How does Elisha solve the problem?

5. *2 Kings 4:42-44*

Describe the setting and the miracle recorded in these verses.

6. *2 Kings 8:1-6*

This follow-up story on the Shunammite woman and her son takes place about seven years after her son was restored to life. We include it here to help tie the two stories together and note how God continues to care for the everyday needs of this family. In addition, commentators note that this episode logically happens before the story of Naaman, Elisha, and Gehazi (lesson 8), in which Gehazi is punished with an infection of leprosy (see 2 Kings 5:27).

a. How did Elisha protect the Shunammite woman and her family from the famine?

b. What leads the king to help the woman receive back her land?

Questions for Reflection

What do these stories teach us about God?

Which of the stories in these passages is most meaningful to you? Why?

Lesson 8

2 Kings 5

"There Is a Prophet in Israel"

Additional Related Scriptures

1 Kings 20; 22:29-40
2 Kings 3:1
Ephesians 4:15
Colossians 4:5
1 Peter 3:15

Introductory Notes

The story of Naaman's healing may seem simple and straightforward at first, but there are several intriguing aspects to this story and its application. As you read the verses of this passage, consider what these people's lives were like. What seems to motivate them? What might they be feeling? What do their futures hold?

Keep in mind that Naaman is a commander of a great enemy army. Consider how you might feel if a high-ranking enemy officer came to a hospital near you for treatment. Note together also that God's mercy and care extend to all peoples. We can all give thanks that God's grace is free and does not depend on financial circumstances, status, or ethnic background.

1. 2 Kings 5:1-7

Note: Ten talents of silver weigh 750 pounds (350 kg); six thousand shekels of gold weigh about 150 pounds (70 kg).

a. Describe Naaman.

b. What does the servant girl propose, and what does Naaman do in response?

c. How does the king of Israel react to the letter from the king of Aram? Why?

2. *2 Kings 5:8-12*

a. What message does Elisha send to the king of Israel?

b. What message does Elisha send to Naaman?

c. What had Naaman expected?

3. *2 Kings 5:13-19a*

a. How do Naaman's servants reason with him? How does Naaman respond?

b. What does Naaman do next, and why?

c. How does Elisha react? Why?

d. In response, what is Naaman's request? What does it mean?

4. *2 Kings 5:19b-27*

   a. What is Gehazi's plan, and how does he carry it out?

   b. Compare Naaman and Gehazi. Who acts more like a follower of God?

c. What is Gehazi's punishment? How can it serve as a warning to us?

Questions for Reflection

What do we learn about God in this lesson?

What do we learn about ourselves?

Lesson 9

2 Kings 6:1-23

Trusting in God

Additional Related Scriptures

1 Kings 20:1-34; 22:29-40
Daniel 2:19-23
Matthew 5:43-48; 6:28-34
Romans 5:8-11
Hebrews 4:13

Introductory Notes

In our Scriptures for this lesson we have two stories that help us focus on trusting in God. One story shows how God cares about our individual challenges from day to day, and the other shows how God watches over individual believers while also protecting his entire people. In addition, we find here an important message about showing mercy to enemies. As you read through these passages, look for insights and pointers to the message and ministry of Jesus, who came to give his life for us all "when we were God's enemies" (Rom. 5:10), so that "whoever believes in him may have eternal life" (John 3:15).

1. *2 Kings 6:1-7*

   a. What does the company of the prophets want to do? Why?

   b. What problem arises, and how is it solved?

c. How does this miracle show that God works in the many details of our lives?.

2. *2 Kings 6:8-14*

a. How does the king of Israel know where the Arameans are as they move from camp to camp?

b. How does the king of Aram respond?

c. How does the king of Aram try to capture Elisha?

3. *2 Kings 6:15-17*

a. How does Elisha's servant react to the sight of the enemy?

b. What does the servant realize when God answers Elisha's prayer for him?

4. *2 Kings 6:18-23*

a. What happens to the enemy as they advance?

b. Where does Elisha lead them, and why?

c. What does the king of Israel want to do, and what does Elisha tell him instead?

d. Why does the enemy stop attacking Israel?

Questions for Reflection

What do we learn about Elisha from this lesson?

What do we learn about the Lord and how to live as God's people?

In what ways do we change as a result of God's mercy?

Lesson 10

2 Kings 6:24-7:20; 13:20-21

Prophecy and Power

Additional Related Scriptures

Deuteronomy 28

2 Kings 3:1-3, 12-14; 8:7-15; 9:1-13; 13:14-19

Introductory Notes

This lesson focuses mainly on a terrible siege on Samaria, an episode in the life of God's people that again shows God's faithfulness despite the people's unfaithfulness. In this story we see another remarkable event that confirms Elisha as the prophet of the Lord, who brings God's Word to the people for their everyday living. Despite the unfaithfulness of many Israelites around him, Elisha remains faithful, empowered by the Spirit of God. Later we also see that God works life-giving power through this prophet even after Elisha has died.

One of the main teachings to highlight when we study the lives of Elijah and Elisha is that they point to the faithful, obedient life of Jesus, who came to set us free from the oppression of sin and to give us abundant life forever with God. From these stories and in the power of the Holy Spirit we can continue to find inspiration to trust in God and to live faithfully every day.

1. *2 Kings 6:24-31*

    a. Describe the severity of the siege.

    b. Whom does the king of Israel blame for this trouble?

2. *2 Kings 6:32-7:2*

   a. What happens next?

   b. What does the king realize about the disaster?

   c. What message does Elisha bring from the Lord?

3. *2 Kings 7:3-9*

   a. What do the lepers decide to do? Why?

   b. What do they find at the Aramean camp—and then what do they do? Explain.

4. *2 Kings 7:10-16*

a. How does the king interpret the news at first?

b. How does the king find out what has really happened?

c. What do the people do, and what does this tell us about Elisha's prophecy from the Lord?

5. *2 Kings 7:17-20*

How do Elisha's words about the king's officer come true?

6. *2 Kings 13:20-21*

As we reach the end of this study, we focus on a brief passage that notes Elisha's death and a surprising miracle that happens after his death. The intervening chapters of 2 Kings briefly mention some episodes in which Elisha plays a role to fulfill God's words in 1 Kings 19:15-17. In those episodes Elisha anoints two kings—Hazael of Aram, and Jehu of Israel (2 Kings 8:7-15; 9:1-13)—who bring further punishment on Israel for their unfaithfulness.

Scholars estimate that Elisha lived to be more than eighty years old, and throughout his life he continued to live faithfully for the Lord. Even as he suffered from sickness on his deathbed, Elisha prophesied for yet another king of Israel who did not live faithfully (2 Kings 13:12-19).

a. After Elisha has died, why is another body thrown into the prophet's tomb?

b. What happens to that body?

Questions for Reflection

What do we learn about faithfulness in this lesson?

Despite our own failings, what has God accomplished to deliver us?

What evidence of God's deliverance do we see in our own lives?

How can we share this good news with others?

An Invitation

Listen now to what God is saying to you.

You may be aware of things in your life that keep you from coming near to God. You may have thought of God as someone who is unsympathetic, angry, and punishing. You may feel as if you don't know how to pray or how to come near to God.

"But because of his great love for us, God, who is rich in mercy, made us alive with Christ even when we were dead in transgressions—it is by grace you have been saved" (Eph. 2:4-5). Jesus, God's Son, died on the cross to save us from our sins. It doesn't matter where you come from, what you've done in the past, or what your heritage is. God has been watching over you and caring for you, drawing you closer. "You also were included in Christ when you heard the word of truth, the gospel of your salvation" (Eph. 1:13).

Do you want to receive Jesus as your Savior and Lord? It's as simple as A-B-C:

- **A**dmit that you have sinned and that you need God's forgiveness.
- **B**elieve that God loves you and that Jesus has already paid the price for your sins.
- **C**ommit your life to God in prayer, asking the Lord to forgive your sins, nurture you as his child, and fill you with the Holy Spirit.

Prayer of Commitment

Here is a prayer of commitment recognizing Jesus Christ as Savior. If you long to be in a loving relationship with Jesus, pray this prayer. If you have already committed your life to Jesus, use this prayer for renewal and praise.

> Dear God, I come to you simply and honestly to confess that I have sinned, that sin is a part of who I am. And yet I know that you listen to sinners who are truthful before you. So I come with empty hands and heart, asking for forgiveness.
>
> I confess that only through faith in Jesus Christ can I come to you. I confess my need for a Savior, and I thank you, Jesus, for dying on the cross to pay the price for my sins. Father, I ask that you forgive my sins and count me as righteous for Jesus' sake. Remove the guilt that accompanies my sin and bring me into your presence.
>
> Holy Spirit of God, help me to pray, and teach me to live by your Word. Faithful God, help me to serve you faithfully. Make me more like Jesus each day, and help me to share with others the good news of your great salvation. In Jesus' name, Amen.

Bibliography

Barker, Kenneth L., and John R. Kohlenberger III. *Zondervan NIV Bible Commentary.* Grand Rapids, Mich.: Zondervan, 1994.

Elwell, Walter A., ed. *Baker Encyclopedia of the Bible.* Grand Rapids, Mich.: Baker Book House, 1988.

Gray, John. *I and II Kings: A Commentary.* Second edition. The Old Testament Library. Philadelphia: Westminster Press, 1970, 1976.

Guthrie, D., and J. A. Motyer, eds. *The New Bible Commentary: Revised.* Grand Rapids, Mich.: Eerdmans, 1970.

Keil, C. F., and F. Delitzsch. *Commentary on the Old Testament.* Volume III. Grand Rapids, Mich.: Eerdmans, 1975.

NIV Study Bible. Grand Rapids, Mich.: Zondervan, 1985.

Evaluation Questionnaire

DISCOVER ELIJAH AND ELISHA: PROPHETS WITH POWER

As you complete this study, please fill out this questionnaire to help us evaluate the effectiveness of our materials. Please be candid. Thank you.

1. Was this a home group ___ or a church-based ___ program?
   What church?

2. Was the study used for
   ___ a community evangelism group?
   ___ a community faith-nurture group?
   ___ a church Bible study group?

3. How would you rate the materials?

   Study Guide
   ___ excellent ___ very good ___ good ___ fair ___ poor

   Leader Guide
   ___ excellent ___ very good ___ good ___ fair ___ poor

4. What were the strengths?

5. What were the weaknesses?

6. What would you suggest to improve the material?

7. In general, what was the experience of your group?

Your name (optional) ____________________

Address ____________________

____

8. Other comments:

(Please fold, tape, stamp, and mail. Thank you.)

Faith Alive Christian Resources
2850 Kalamazoo Ave. SE
Grand Rapids, MI 49560